A Certain Season

A Certain Season

Season

Poems from the First Half of My Life

Ted Roupas
Drawings by Jeff DeBlasio

outskirts
press

To the memory of my parents
This book is fondly dedicated.

I say — a toast to Mother!
A second toast, to Dad!
Had either missed the other
I would not have been had!

CONTENTS

BETTER LATE THAN NEVER

All poets past whose works I know—
Such names as Shakespeare, Wordsworth, Poe—
In early youth gave ample sign
That theirs would prove a vintage wine.
Then how shall verse from my pen flow?
Shall I some talent hope to show
When, fully formed at twenty-nine,
I've scarcely done a single line?

And yet, to *want* the poet's art
Has got to play no minor part:
Before, I never cared to be
A person that wrote poetry.
Now all at once within my heart
The wish is there to make a start:
The wish—I now have that in me. . . .
As to the talent, we shall see.

KNOW-IT-ALL

Everything I write,
This person labels "trite".
To every word I say,
This person says "cliché".
Could he no trite phrase attack, he'd
Tell me that my *theme* was hackneyed.
Hackneyed, trite, cliché—
This person never learned
These criticisms may
Against themselves be turned.

WORTH POLISHING

"It's not stupid—it's plain idiotic
  So to labor. Keep moving ahead!"
So you tell me. You say I'm neurotic,
  But I call it high standards instead.

For each tiny detail's of the essence,
  And a single small word out of place
Can distract like a glaring excrescence
On an otherwise beautiful face.

No, you can't put a price on perfection:
  One bright diamond, all fire, is enough
And worth more than a whole bland collection
  Of dull specimens, still in the rough.

Then take heart—all misgivings abolish
  That this diamond's too slight and too small,
And continue to cut, grind, and polish
  Till it sparkles the brightest of all.

COMING OF SPRING

When all at once along the trail
  No longer is it snowing,
And one feels not the winter's gale
  But warmer breezes blowing,

And one wears still one's winter wrap
  But takes away the lining
Because, awake from six months' nap,
  The sun is once more shining,

Then in the earth's hard crust of ice
  A tiny crack starts growing.
It spreads—it's gone: when one looks twice
  A thousand streams are flowing!

A robin on a branch above
  Gives voice to sudden yearning—
And as for me, to thoughts of love
  I find my fancy turning.

RAINY SPRING

At times it seemed catastrophe was coming:
  No sooner had the ice begun to melt
Than grimly, with a sound like fateful drumming,
  The rain, the dreadful rain, began to pelt.
The wet kept on day after dreary day
And everything was damp, and cold, and gray.

The days went by, and then the rain grew stronger
  As if to guarantee impending doom.
Then, just when I could bear the rain no longer,
  A patch of sunlight fell inside my room . . .
And when I next looked out upon the scene
Everything was fresh, and lush, and green!

LATE LETTER

A missive from my missus!
  High time I had some word—
I can't believe how long
  It's been, since last I heard.

That's right—the last I heard
  Was three full days ago!
Why has she kept me waiting
  So long, I'd like to know?

Yes, that I'd like to know.
  Just what has she been doing?
I'm ready to suspect
  Some mischief has been brewing.

Some mischief has been brewing,
  But why? What did I do?
Fool, I let her wander,
  Thinking that she'd be true.

I thought that she'd be true,
  I should have known better—
She's fallen for another,
  She'll say so in this letter.

I'll read it in this letter,
  Her coolness there will show. . .
"My darling, do you miss me?
  I love you, miss you so."

"I love you, miss you so."
  Then everything's all right!
My angel, you still love me.
  You gave me such a fright!

You gave me such a fright:
  Please, love, while you're away
Do not forget to write
  Each and every day!

ETERNAL RECURRENCE

Since once we met, again we'll meet,
For all is destined to repeat.
And so we'll never stop, you see—
We'll keep on meeting, endlessly.
That, anyway, was *Nietzsche's* claim,
Which he considered welcome news—
And I'm inclined to feel the same,
Look forward to our rendezvous.

A BACHELOR'S LIFE FOR ME

Skillets' clang and dishes' clatter—
  Call you that felicity?
Baby's cry and lady's chatter—
  Voilà domesticity!
No, the bachelor sees things clearly,
  His the only life for me;
Peace of mind he values dearly,
  Vive his tranquillity!

Look around at friends and neighbors
  Trapped like flies on sticky tape,
Notice their heroic labors
  As they struggle to escape.
No, there's precious little gained in
  Taking vows, that much I see—
Not for me, to be enchained in
  Fetters of fidelity!

Many men at first enchanted
  With their wives have later found,
Love that blooms when freely granted
  Withers when by duty bound.
No, I won't go near the altar,
  Love is bond enough for me—
Then if love should ever falter,
  At that moment I'll be free!

See the victims of illusion
 Hurry to embrace their doom.
All things point to this conclusion:
 At a wedding, don't be groom!
Still, I've known resolve to soften—
 While I swear defiantly,
"I won't marry her!", I often
 Wonder, *Will she marry me?*

PREOCCUPIED PROFESSOR

As I before my class now rise
And open up my lecture book,
I see before me lovely eyes
All trained on me with eager look.

I start with some amusing quips
To make my students feel at ease,
And as reward the smiling lips
Of pretty girls my senses please.

While I discourse on views and *isms*
With flourish and dramatic show,
My eyes delight in swelling bosoms—
Oh sweet young girls, I love you so!

Midst solemn tones and thoughtful sighs,
Discussing theories of the Good,
I catch a glimpse of shapely thighs
That thrills my heart and warms my blood.

Would you not be surprised indeed
At all the things that you would find
If you, dear girls, right now could read
The thoughts in your professor's mind?

WEIGHT WATCHER

As I survey the crowded beach
I'm suddenly deprived of speech:
I notice, on a nearby mat,
A great, enormous mound of fat.
This grant me, Lord, I Thee beseech:
Please help me keep my belly flat—
I pray that I may never reach
The stage at which I look like *that!*

LINES TO ACCOMPANY GIFT ON ST. PATRICK'S DAY

This St. Patrick's Day think green
Underneath and in between:
Not just what the public sees,
What by you alone is seen.
So attired, yourself you'll please—
And the one that gives you these.

FIRST EXPOSURE

Of the sun
I'm afraid.
Time to run
For the shade!

MASTERY MAKES DEMANDS

To those convinced that *Nero's* fault was great
In fiddling while the city round him burned,
I say that he might well have been concerned
But mastery makes demands—all else can wait.

As more than one has felt: each day out late
Discussing virtue, *Socrates* returned
To face Xanthippe's wrath, he having spurned
All goals except to get the matter straight.

The rhymester too: I know the feeling well—
That nothing counts except the rhyme be clean.
Damn! Even now the world can go to hell
Before I'll quit! By God, and though it mean
The final loss of my immortal soul
I'll fit that squarish peg in that round hole!

INCONVENIENT ATTRIBUTE

How I love to see the pretty girls along the beach!
　Up and down I walk along the shore.
One by one I pass them by and want to say to each,
　"Pretty girl, it's you that I adore."

Look at that one straight ahead, observe her lovely face;
　Never was there goddess more divine.
Tall and slim she seems the very paragon of grace—
　Ah, if I could only make her mine!

What a sexy kitten's this—I'd not object to her;
　Cute she is, and cuddly as can be.
Lovingly to stroke her back and listen to her purr—
　That would be delightful, you'll agree.

There's one young and tender with the look of sweet
　Swelling like a bud about to bloom.　　　　　sixteen,
If I could I'd pick her now while still a little green,
　Take her home to blossom in my room.

There's another farther on, a little more mature;
　Notice her sophisticated air.
Strikingly attractive she's had many men I'm sure—
　Would that their good fortune I might share!

Thus as I proceed along, my eyes delight in each—
　Yet without a word I pass on by.
Countless pretty girls, and all alone I walk the beach—
　What an inconvenience to be shy!

THE FERRY

The wind's blowing lightly
   From water to land;
The sun's shining brightly,
   The weather is grand.
A cloud in slow motion
   Traverses the sky,
While waves on the ocean
   Skip merrily by.

And rowboats and sailboats
   Enliven the view:
Gay patches of color
   On a background of blue.
When the scene is so cheerful,
   So perfect the day,
Can it be any wonder
   My spirits are gay?

A small crowd has gathered
   Alongside the dock;
They're awaiting the ferry,
   Due soon by the clock.
A mood of elation
   Prevails in the air:
When it's summer vacation
   One hasn't a care.

A girl with a tan
　Is expecting her beau,
An anxious young man
　Hopes some lady will show,
There's one who looks forward
　To seeing a friend,
Another has simply
　Some free time to spend.

A handful are walking
　Around and around,
While others are talking
　To friends they have found.
Excitement is mounting,
　One watches it grow
As folks begin counting
　The minutes to go . . .

But look—in the distance
　A small speck of white!
It's moving—the ferry
　Has come into sight!
The shape of her figure
　Is visible now;
You can see her round sides
　And the line of her prow.

She's fast getting closer
　And soon will be here.
Now faint sounds of music
　Occur to the ear:
The band that she carries
　Has started to play
As *Beer Barrel Polka*
　Floats over the bay.

Next minute one catches
　The smell of her fumes
As larger and larger
　And larger she looms.
Her whistle now blows—
　People jump at the blast!
She draws ever closer,
　She puts in at last.

And there at the railing
　The passengers stand,
All frantically hailing
　Those waiting on land.
Appearing before us
　Thus all in a row
They seem like the chorus
　In some Broadway show.

Directly the crew
　Begins rushing about,
The engines are silenced,
　The ropes are tossed out,
The gangplank is lifted
　And slid into place—
Now eagerly down it
　The passengers race . . .

And suddenly people
　Are greeting their friends;
To all those arriving
　Warm welcome extends.
In loving embraces
　Now sweethearts unite;
The smiles on their faces
　Express their delight.

But who is that waving
And smiling at me?
I know well enough—
It's my darling I see.
When the ferry comes in
I have always a treat
But when darling is on it
My joy is complete.

REFLECTIVE AFTERNOON

The sky is one expanse of vivid blue
Against which seagulls wheel and dip and soar;
Beneath, the water's more a greenish hue
Where seaweed rises from the ocean floor.
The surf comes rolling in with muffled roar,
Advances up the beach and then recedes.
It leaves behind it, cast upon the shore,
Smooth, colored stones among the drying weeds,
That sparkle in the sun like shiny, flashing beads.

Preoccupied I revel in her eyes
As up and down her arm I run my hand;
How beautiful she looks as there she lies
Bikini-clad, her body lithe and tanned.
After awhile she has a mind to stand
So as to better gather in the view:
The washed-up stones lie shining in the sand—
And she, not having anything to do,
Announces her intent to go collect a few.

Bending to me with reassuring smile
She kisses me, then gaily walks away;
I raise myself and look at her awhile
To see in what direction she will stray.
My eyes take in a host of people; they
Lie sprawling on their blankets all around.
The beach is one bright, colorful display:
Red, yellow, green and purple all abound
And here and there a more unusual shade is found.

The people too—how unalike in shade!
Not only shade but also shape and size.
How differently each one of us is made!
Why? How does such variety arise?
And suddenly it's plain—I realize
We people on our blankets stretched or curled
Are like those stones that near and far one spies:
As they by chance upon the beach are hurled
So we are cast upon the shore of the wide world . . .

And chance, that settles what shall see the light,
Leads everywhere to inequality—
As some among those stones are gay and bright
And others drab and colorless, so we
Are blessed at birth in varying degree:
One is endowed with talent, beauty, brains,
Another as it happens lacks all three—
And if that soul feels cheated and complains,
There's no response, no voice that comforts or explains.

And he who, discontented with his lot,
Angry at Fate and envious at heart,
Wishes that he had been what he is not
—healthy and strong, confident, daring, smart,
Athletic, graceful, skilled in every art,
Handsome of figure, beautiful of face—
Who wishes himself thus altered from the start
Wishes that there in fact had been no trace
Of him at all, but someone different in his place.

When I reflect on people that I know,
I can't but ask myself, What sort am I?
Not anyone exceptional, although
A few have thought me so—I don't know why:
An ordinary, average kind of guy
Who always acts according to the rule,
Who sits and studies books, afraid to try
And change the world, who stayed too long in school
And finally ended up—an educated fool . . .

Who played the usual academic game,
Receiving in due course his PhD,
Then took a road well traveled and became
—what else?—an academic (you'll agree
The job has merit: safe as safe can be
With all the leisure anyone requires) . . .
Who now, however, gazing at the sea,
The sky, the sand, those gleaming stones, desires
To do some grander thing before his time expires.

Be realistic now and face the truth:
I haven't what it takes for that, it's plain;
A person who was average in his youth
And well beyond is certain to remain
Average right to the end. A lot of pain,
Frustration, ridicule are all I'd get
From trying to be more; I stand to gain
The most by simply being myself. And yet—
My not being more is something that I still regret.

But here she comes again: her far-off smile
Gives promise of some treasure from the shore!
The girl has been collecting all this while—
And now from her cupped hands proceed to pour
Colorful stones, as many as a score;
These, dipped anew to make them shine, attest
The ocean's wealth. . . . But still, from that rich store
Acquired by her on her successful quest
There's one that right away stands out from all the rest:

A stone which, dipped and held against the sun,
Is lit within by his bright, piercing rays
As by an inner light; through which there run
Intricate, swirling, gilded passageways
That merge and separate. The more I gaze
At that interior suddenly revealed
To view—the more my busy eye surveys
Its careful, rich design till now concealed—
The more I marvel nature should such treasures yield.

And such a treasure's she—her female form
Arousing total wonder, her smooth face
Compelling love, those large brown eyes as warm
And luminous as that lit stone! Each grace
Possessed by any member of the race
Humanity, is found in her; in her
All lovely features have their meeting place—
For elsewhere too such qualities occur
Yet not all in the same location as it were.

Freely I tell her what I think. At this
She kisses me and whispers in my ear,
"I love you," then bestows a further kiss
As if to demonstrate that she's sincere.
Pulling me to the blanket now, the dear
Enfolds me in her arms; completely drowned
In feeling we lie clasped together here,
Oblivious to every sight or sound
Impinging on us from the noisy world around.

The afternoon wears on and still we stay
Like this; above, the sun continues bright.
I think how greatly I've enjoyed the day—
And yet I'm certain I'll enjoy the night
Still more. Did not the girl just now invite
Me over for the evening? In her eyes
Do I not read a promise of delight
Unmatched on earth? Oh yes, I recognize
That look of hers, I know quite well what it implies!

Of all the marvelous things that chance creates
—people or stones—does anything excel
A lovely woman, whose amazing traits
Not only thrill the senses but compel
The heart and entire soul to thrill as well:
A woman soft and gentle, warm and kind—
Yet one untamed, in whom wild urges dwell . . .
A woman such as might have been designed
By a supremely great, all-comprehending Mind?

And such is she—a woman that seems sent
From heaven! Then how ridiculous that I
Should lapse into self-pity and lament
My average gifts! I ought to raise a cry
Of joy, not disappointment, to the sky—
Happy that one so dear should simply be,
Happier still that somehow (Who knows why?)
A woman so superior as she
Should nonetheless see fit to give her love to me!

BOYS AND BEES

Johnny is back
  From raiding the hive;
Fierce the attack
  But he will survive.

Dad, who knows life
  And quoting enjoys,
Says to his wife,
  "Well, boys will be boys."

Mom, who with Dad
  On this much agrees,
Hastens to add,
  "And bees will be bees."

LIVE AND LET LIVE

One summer day just sitting
  And gazing at the land,
I suddenly looked down to see
  A hornet on my hand.

It crawled around my fingers
  As through me went a chill;
I watched its path with bated breath
  And kept completely still.

And then it left, its visit
  An innocent caprice. . . .
Would only we let others be,
  The world would be at peace!

PASSING MOOD

The sky shows blue. . . . A drop appears:
Dark clouds collect, it starts to pour.
The clouds disperse, the weather clears:
The sky's its same old self, once more.

DOUBLE RAINBOW

My heart leaps up when I behold
  A rainbow shining bright.
It leaps anew to see unfold
  A second band of light.

The second, still with reds and blues,
  Is fainter than the first;
Identical its whispered hues,
  In order, though, reversed.

Resembling what? An afterglow,
  A faint, reflected bliss
Wherein reversed are high and low—
  The life to follow this?

IMPORTANCE OF TIMING

The wave rose up, and she, her timing right,
Rose with it. Having got herself on top
She rode it in, as buoyant and as light
As foam—till she came sliding to a stop.

Back out, she met another, which she strove
To mount—too late! Suddenly overhead
The monstrous shape came crashing down and drove
Her hard aground and left her nearly dead.

> Yes, timing's of the essence:
>   You let the moment pass,
> No longer do you ride the wave—
>   The wave rides you. Alas!

AT THE SKI RESORT
or WHERE THE PROBLEM LIES

This mountain is one girl whose snowy breast
I stroke as does a novice, clumsily.
She graciously consents to being caressed—
My problem is: I don't know how to ski.

That girl, by contrast, frustrates all my hopes
Of getting her to give herself to me.
My problem's gaining access to her slopes—
I know as well as any how to ski.

KEEPING WARM ON A COLD NIGHT
TO MARY

Outside the flakes are flying
   And drifting deep,
As inside I am trying
   To fall asleep.
The temperature is dropping
   To record lows,
And where it will be stopping
   God only knows!

An icy draft is hitting
   My legs and feet—
I might as well be sitting
   Out on the street.
Beneath the quilts I snuggle
   To raise some heat.
In vain my desperate struggle—
   Like ice the sheet!

In bitter, frigid weather
   That chills the bone,
It's better two together
   Than one alone.
All sleep is being denied me
   By this night's storm—
Were you but here beside me
   To keep me warm!

HOLIDAY TOAST!

Wishing you a Christmas merry,
  Let's now toast this happy hour!
May there always be a cherry
  Garnishing your whisky sour!
May the new year be like satin
  —never rough but always smooth—
And when mixing your Manhattan
  May you have the right *vermoothe!*

Rate of change is supersonic—
  Gone the old, the new is in!
One thing, though, won't change: with tonic
  We shall always take our gin!
But to get you feeling frisky
  May your New Year's glass contain
Nothing mixed with gin or whisky—
  May your drink be pure champagne!

NEW YEAR'S RESOLUTIONS

To rise at break of dawn,
  Not lie sleeping half the day—
If this laziness goes on
  I'll have slept my life away!

In the future to take care
  That I always look my best;
To make sure I comb my hair
  And to watch the way I'm dressed;

To eat wisely—in my diet
  Wholesome dishes to include;
At the table to keep quiet
  When my mouth is full of food;

To stay physically fit
  And to exercise as planned,
Not interminably sit
  With some gadget in my hand;

Never weakly dodge and swerve,
  Aim directly at the goal;
Never, ever lose my nerve
  But be always in control;

Not to merely seek position
  (That's a race the rest may run),
Yet to welcome recognition
  For a job that's been well done;

To be sensitive, not blind,
    To the other's point of view;
At all times to bear in mind
    That the other's human too;

Truth and wisdom to pursue
    With a mind and spirit bold;
To be open to the new
    Yet to not neglect the old;

For life's blessings to be glad,
    On misfortune not to dwell—
For if much there is that's bad
    There is much that's good as well;

Not to let myself grow jaded
    Or by cynics get beguiled,
See the world instead unfaded
    With the freshness of a child . . .

For the world is full of beauty
    (Never mind what doubters say),
And it seems to me our duty
    To enjoy it while we may;

To be cheerful and serene,
    Smile and trust the Lord above;
To make sure my thoughts are clean
    And especially—to love;

In the possibility
    Of man's greatness to believe
And before I die, to see
    That some small thing I achieve;

To remain to these goals true,
  What discomfort it involve—
All these things to be or do
  For the new year I resolve.

And if none can keep a vow
  Such as this, that aims so high,
I declare right here and now
  I at least intend to try!

TO ROSE

Oh Rosie, when we walk beside the pond
On days when spring has touched the land
And this our little place
Is filled with grace,
Then you are like the warmth
Of sun and warm air on my face:
Your presence softly felt and bringing peace.

TO ROSE, AFTER SHE LEFT

Ah me, how much I miss you here,
    I'm lonesome as can be . . .
And yet it's sweet, my Rosie dear,
    To know you think of me.

And as you roam the wide world through,
    You too may always know
My thoughts each day will follow you
    Wherever you may go.

SEASONS' GREETINGS

Home at last, two weary skiers!
  Damp and chilled we reach our door.
Walking in, we're met by flowers
  Smiling in a bright décor.

There beside a spray of holly,
  Flanked by windows piled with snow,
Lovely, full, perfumed and frilly,
  Birthday roses warmly glow.

Fresh as morning, young and tender,
  Nodding from across the room,
Modest, pure, erect and slender,
  Paperwhite narcissus bloom.

Coiled in wreaths of twining branches,
  Helping make the scene complete,
Bearing fruit in showy bunches—
  Orange-and-yellow bittersweet.

So it is each time we enter:
  Warmed and cheered we greet them all—
Greet with gladdened hearts, in winter,
  Winter, summer, spring and fall.

LONELY YEAR

A year has passed since we two hand in hand
Across the meadow walked our little way,
Rejoicing in the beauty of the land
All fresh and blooming in the month of May . . .

A year in which when summer's sun grew hot
I went and stood beneath the maple tree
But felt no comfort in that shady spot
Since you were not there standing next to me . . .

A year in which the bright display of fall,
Whose splendid colors flamed beneath clear skies,
Held hardly any charm for me at all
Since missing was the color of your eyes . . .

A year in which when winter finally came
With numbing cold and snow-propelling storm,
It spread a bitter chill throughout my frame
Without you snuggling close to keep me warm . . .

And so the year has come around to spring.
Again it's May, and flowers bloom anew.
Again life stirs—bees buzz and songbirds sing.
And I? I walk our way and think of you.

ON HIS SIMULTANEOUSLY BEING JILTED
AND NOTICING HIS HAIR STARTING TO THIN

I don't know why I'm so dejected:
   My sweetheart left, it's true,
But this I rather half expected—
   It's really nothing new;
I've known the end of love's sweet madness
   A dozen times or more . . .
And yet, today I feel a sadness
   I've never felt before.

What circumstance could cause this feeling?
   Did I love her the best?
Were her ways so much more appealing
   Than those of all the rest?
If she seems now the one loved dearest
   Once others seemed so too. . . .
Perhaps it's just that what lies nearest
   Looms greatest in our view.

I'm downcast for a different reason:
   These wrinkles in my brow
Serve notice of a change of season—
   Yes, spring is over now.
My life's no longer just beginning—
   It's no use to pretend:
When once your hair has started thinning
   You're halfway to the end.

Not mine the jilted lover's sorrow—
  That's not what it's about;
For love will come again tomorrow,
  I haven't any doubt.
But now my youth is finally over—
  It's this I'm feeling, then! . . .
For youth, which gladly I'd recover,
  Will never come again.

DISCONNECTED

Beneath this dome are two of me.
  Of late I've grown disgusted:
With what I say, I disagree—
  I simply can't be trusted.

The cure, on which I now rely,
  Is something called prevention:
I recognize my voice, and I
  Refuse to pay attention.

With listening to myself I'm done!
  A different game I'm playing. . . .
I wonder, now does *anyone*
  Know what on earth I'm saying?

EXASPERATION

Every morning it's the same old story—
Now where the hell is my other zori?

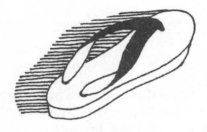

LIMBURGER

Is not the thing a paradox—
   Thing real and not fictitious:
A cheese that smells like dirty socks
   Yet tastes downright delicious?

GRAPE SNACK

She stems a grape,
Then pops the smooth ellipsoid
Into her mouth.
From her pursed lips
Aimed low
Three seeds shoot down
And bounce against the plate.

She glances up:
Her fingers pluck another grape.
Again the stem,
Again the mouth
Opened to receive—
Then three more seeds. . . .

In the end the plate,
A mound of stems and seeds,
Two smiling lips that glisten,
And a row of teeth—
Small, white, and even.

DOWNED ROBIN

Downfall of robin,
Too young to fly
—another week, perhaps—
One leg dangling as loose
As a key on chain.

Alive nevertheless,
In drizzle it was found
And taken by me,
Provider of dry warmth,
Soft bedding and good worms.

And so good night:
May your pain abate
And you recover
To enjoy the world,
Though I doubt you'll ever have
But one good leg.

But pain,
Strange bed,
And I ≠ mother:
The change was all too much,
And in the morning
—so bright and beautiful a day!—
The poor thing limp,
Eyes closed up
Forever.

ZELINSKY ON KANDINSKY

When asked what he thought of *Kandinsky,*
Said a chap by the name of *Zelinsky,*
   "Well, I ain't much on art
   But to speak from the heart
I prefer *Leonardo Davinsky.*"

ON INVESTIGATING THEORIES OF ART

I've read enough! This endless series
Of grandiose aesthetic theories
At first intrigues, but finally wearies.

It's true, as *Plato* wisely said,
A pictured bed is not a bed:
The picture's something else instead.

But is it something quite unreal,
As he appeared to also feel?
To me, that view has less appeal.

Some lines in *Aristotle* state
That artists only imitate.
But do they therefore not create?

That they do not would seem to follow—
A thesis that's a little hollow
And one that I find hard to swallow.

Some tout, as drama's one firm base,
The unities of time and place:
These hold, they say, in every case.

So *Horace* taught, so too *Boileau*—
And yet, as many dramas show,
This view of theirs just isn't so.

The ancients leave—let's move ahead.
Aesthetic pleasure, *Kant* has said,
Is totally disinterested.

I wonder, does he mean to claim
That people's tastes are all the same?
If so, his grounds seem rather lame.

At once *Romantics* come along
—a tribe about a thousand strong—
Proclaiming Kant had got it wrong.

The artist in her work reveals
Essentially the way she feels:
Emotion's that in which she deals.

Yet wait a minute, don't let's rush—
When feeling starts to well and gush
The end result's not art, but mush.

Wrote *Bell,* who took the world by storm:
Not feeling is the key, but form.
At last, perhaps, we're getting warm?

And if we are? The truth's belated—
My interest has evaporated;
I'm quite exhausted, as I've stated.

As *Whitman,* when he heard that dry
Astonomer tell how and why,
Got up, walked out, and scanned the sky,

So I, grown tired and sick at heart
Of what art theorists' works impart,
Would view unbriefed some work of art.

THE SHOW

I can hardly believe that it's over,
  It all went by so fast.
The show, so long in the future,
  Is now a thing of the past.
The efforts I gave to preparing
  Seem suddenly all in vain . . .
For what is there left one can point to?
  Only the sets remain.

I spent hours on the proper inflection
  Of just one little phrase,
And to do a whole line to perfection
  Took a total of several days;
For weeks, from the moment I started,
  I ran through the words in my head. . . .
The curtains no sooner had parted,
  In a twinkling the words had been said.

How I practiced and practiced and practiced
  That one very difficult song!
No matter how often I tried it
  It always sounded wrong.
With time the mistakes were corrected,
  I became quite adept at the tune—
I never, no never expected
  The piece would be over so soon.

At first, when I tried to add dancing,
  The trouble I had with my feet!
Resolved, I eventually trained them
  To move in time with the beat.
And now that the whole thing is over
  Will I ever again have the chance
To sing that particular number,
  To dance that particular dance?

Yet supposing I won't, still I wonder
  If it all was entirely a waste.
Was it really for naught? No, by thunder!
  How absurd: Were my efforts misplaced?
The performance could not have gone better,
  It was virtually free of flaws . . .
And oh, the thrill that went through me
  When I heard that final applause!

THEN AND NOW

When I was still a youngster
　My father said to me,
"When you become an adult
　What do you want to be?

A much-admired physician,
　A doctor, an MD?"
A life spent helping others
　Seemed worthiest to me.

"Or might you be a lawyer
　And charge a kingly fee?"
To make a lot of money—
　That too appealed to me.

"A businessman, the leader
　Of some big company?"
Not only wealth, but power—
　That also I could see.

"A scholarly professor
　With many a degree?"
Devote myself to knowledge—
　That too was fine with me.

He'd never have suggested
　Pursuing poetry,
And anyway, a poet
　I'd not have cared to be.

And now that I'm an adult
Of nearly thirty-three
I'm no respected doctor—
At least, I'm no MD.

I'm not a clever lawyer
Who draws a handsome fee,
And neither wealth nor power
Seems now in store for me.

I'm just a plain professor
With one advanced degree,
Who wishes he could prosper
By writing poetry.

INSCRIPTON IN BOOK *THE WALL STREET JUNGLE*
GIFT TO FATHER

Wall Street is a pathless jungle:
Missed, the forest for the trees.
Many smart investors bungle—
May you not be one of these!

EARTHBOUND

For hours on end I've racked my brains
　And still the words sound wrong.
What's the use of all my pains?
　I haven't the gift of song.

I keep on wishing I could fly
　And weren't to earth so bound.
In vain—no matter how hard I try
　I can't get off the ground.

With cautious step I inch my way
　In hopes I'm on the track—
As often as not, to my dismay
　I'm on a cul-de-sac.

And when I try to soar in space
　I only trip and fall.
Perhaps I'm wrong, if that's the case,
　To even try at all?

As when the earth revives in spring
　Sap rises in the tree,
So when my heart is moved to sing
　Let song arise in me.

In perfect measures sweet and clear
　Let song in time come out . . .
As on the branches buds appear
　And leaves, when ready, sprout.

BITTERSWEET KISS

Oh the joy at last to kiss you!
Oh the heartache knowing then
—darling Mary!—how I'd miss you
Till the chance to kiss again.

ON THE SAYING "KNOWLEDGE IS POWER"

"Knowledge is power," said Bacon. And indeed
Some knowledge is: it has its uses. Still,
What uses? Science expands the power to kill.
Hazards abound where some discoveries lead.

Untended, knowledge burgeons like a weed
Whose galloping vines go wild and overspill
All bounds. Contain it, then, and let it fill
Some vacancy, some pressing, genuine need!

The knowledge I'm most eager to pursue
Is power all right—the gentle power to please.
It's knowing all the ins and outs of you
And what it takes to make you feel at ease
And feel like heaven has just come into view
And sigh, a sudden weakness in your knees.

WEDDING VOW (FOR BRIDES)

I, _____, do take you, _____,
To be my lawfully wedded husband:
To have and to hold,
Be you young, be you old;
For better, for worse;
Be you sweet, or perverse;
For richer, for poorer;
Be you less sure, or surer;
In sickness and in health;
In poverty and wealth;
In good times and bad;
Be you gentleman, or cad;
Teetotaler or drinker;
A gem, or a stinker;
Lowbrow or thinker;
At peace and at war;
Should it prove you're a bore;
Should it prove that you snore;
Be you lover or dud;
Limp, or a stud;
Kind or cruel;
Wise, or a fool;
Clumsy or able;
Should you belch at the table;
Should your manners be super
Or you swear like a trooper;
Should you sit up or slouch;
Be you fun, or a grouch;
Should your pipe stain the couch;
Should your feet perspire;
Your conversation tire;

Be you fat or thin;
Should your breath smell of gin;
Be you thoughtful in bed
Or unthoughtful instead;
Be you tiny or huge;
Be you Santa or Scrooge;
A lion or a mouse;
A lamb or a louse;
Clever or dumb;
Responsive, or numb;
A doll, or a crumb;
A prince or a pauper;
Flop, or show-stopper;
Be you shallow or deep;
Spendthrift, or cheap;
Neat guy, or creep;
Be you weakling or hunk;
Kitten or skunk;
Fit or flabby;
Quiet or gabby;
Solemn or flip;
Darling, or drip;
To love and obey
Be whatever you may:
Be your spine like spaghetti;
Your brain like confetti;
Be you smelly and sweaty;
A crook and a liar;
Complainer and crier;
Be you old at heart;
Be you stupid—or smart . . .
Till death us do part.

ANCIENT PHILOSOPHICAL SCHOOL

Long ago, in times Paleozoic,
Rose a school led by *Zeno the Stoic*.
  First came virtue, they reckoned,
  While pleasure came second.
Their refusal to grumble: heroic.

FELLOW NAMED SLOAN

There once was a fellow named Sloan—
A neurotic who played the trombone.
  He was troubled inside
  By the thought of his slide
And could not leave the damn thing alone.

SICK JOKE

As a joke once, a man spread a rumor
That a friend had developed a tumor.
  When they asked, "Is it cancer?"
  "It *is*" was his answer—
He had rather a *sick* sense of humor.

MAN FROM OAHU

There once was a man from Oahu—
An uncouth sort of chap, a real *yahoo*.
  In a restaurant one night
  He got into a fight
When the waiter scoffed, "What's *mahu-mahu*?"

THE CONSPIRATORS

Lights in the distance, music and laughter—
  We listen, surrounded by night.
The people are all at the carnival, dancing—
  We see, but we stay out of sight.

Not for us is the dance band's loud music
  Or the tom-tom's relentless beat.
Not for us, the whirl of bright costumes
  Or the stamping of frenzied feet.

Unnoticed we move back and forth on the outskirts
  And this is our only thought:
We'll be beaten and tortured and made to die slowly
  If ever we're caught.

FELLOW NAMED MICK

There once was a fellow named Mick
Who was listed as *I. M. A. Dick.*
  He had ribbings aplenty—
  By the time he was twenty
His skin had become pretty thick.

NINE-YEAR-OLD LASSIE

On the outskirts of old Tallahassee
Lived a dad and a nine-year-old lassie.
  Told to tidy her shelf
  She said, "Do it yourself."
Thought her father, *By God, but she's sassy!*

GIRL WHO LOVED SLIME

There once was a girl who loved slime.
She would play with the stuff all the time.
  She would shout, amid squeals,
  "I just love how this feels—
The sensation is simply sublime!"

FELLOW NAMED LUCAS

There once was a fellow named Lucas
Who was plagued by an excess of mucus.
  He would sniffle and spray
  And behave in a way
For which there was just no *excucus.*

PROVINCETOWN, CAPE COD

Compelled by fate
Each goes his way—
Some folks are straight
And some are gay.

MAN FROM CAPE COD

Among people I've met, the most odd
Was a man that I met on Cape Cod:
  He had long, stringy hair
  And a beard down to *there*—
When I asked him his name he said *God*.

UP A TREE

What you doing up there,
You ridiculous cat?
On the ground so agile
—stalking, springing, pivoting, sprinting—
Look at you now:
High in the oak tree you crouch,
Immobile.
In your element the terror
Of squirrels and birds,
Now the butt of their ridicule.
Unafraid, squirrels run back and forth
On a neighboring branch;
Birds perch
Only inches away,
All laughing.

It's no use closing your eyes,
Pretending you're somewhere else.
Sooner or later you'll just have to face it:
You're up a tree!

What made you climb so high?
Were you chased by a dog,
In your panic forgetting
Dogs can't climb trees at all?
Were you chasing a squirrel,
In your eagerness forgetting
Squirrels are built
To scamper about in trees
While you are not?

Did you never consider
What an awkward predicament
You were fast getting into
As higher and higher you climbed?

If only you had stopped
A quarter of the way up,
You could have jumped
And been none the worse for the fall.
You can't jump now!

I hear you meowing,
But what can I do?
I'm even less adept than you
At getting about in trees:
I couldn't begin to climb the trunk
Of that tall oak.

I know what you're feeling, poor thing—
I'm up a tree myself.
I can't begin to imagine
How I'm going to get down.
Money. Where will I find the money?
Help—I need help—
Please, somebody!
Won't somebody come to my rescue?

I hear you meowing,
I hear you crying "Help!"
All right, all right,
Be patient awhile.
I'm going to canvas the neighborhood:
Somebody must have a ladder.

GREEK CONNECTION

There's something I like about you,
A feature of yours that well suits
A desire I've been feeling anew—
The desire to return to my roots.

Before my Greek grandmother died
The family—my uncles and aunts—
Would gather around at her side
To talk and to sing and to dance.

Although they would mostly speak Greek,
Of which I surmised not a word,
I'd listen for hours to them speak,
Entranced by the sounds that I heard.

The cousins would come along too:
I recall, if my memory checks,
That though Greek was a language they knew,
They spoke English and talked about sex—

The ones who were older, I mean,
Such as Ernie and George and two Nick's.
The others, like me and Irene,
Could not have been much over six.

When discussion was through we'd repair
To the table, in order to dine;
Ambrosia awaited us there,
And our nectar was retsina wine.

My grandmother used to make bread
And pastries with honey and spice;
At Easter the eggs were all red,
And the lamb yielded many a slice.

It seems everything good disappears—
The family has long since dispersed;
The wellsprings that nourished those years
Have long ceased to quench any thirst.

I had almost lost sight of my past,
The recovery of which I now seek. . . .
You remind me, Faye, at long last
Of what it is to be Greek.

Yet for all that, my feelings are such
That there must be some other thing too—
Were you Irish or English or Dutch
I'd still like you as well as I do!

TO FAYE

Faye, what spell is this you're working,
  What concealed black magic, Faye?
Duties, errands, chores I'm shirking,
  Lost in dreams I pass the day.
My appointments I'm not keeping
And at nighttime I'm not sleeping:
  Dream by day, awake by night—
  Clearly something isn't right!

At the time when you first met me
  Life was calm and even-paced,
Nothing able to upset me—
  Now it seems that's all erased.
Only yesterday contented
Suddenly I feel tormented:
  Pity one who feels unwell—
  Faye, release me from your spell!

No, do not. Whatever duty
  You demand, I'll gladly do;
To such rare, exotic beauty
  I surrender through and through.
But you'll pay for my devotion—
Now I brew the magic potion:
  Cauldron bubble, fire burn—
  Feel my magic, Faye, in turn!

RESTLESS

The moon shone bright, I held you tight,
   The time had come for mating. . . .
Then suddenly you said good night—
   I found that most frustráting!
Now all I do is think of you:
   I'll not get any rest
Until you're with me all night through,
   Against me tightly pressed.

GREETINGS TO RUTH, NIKKI,
AND ESPECIALLY FAYE

Greetings, Faye and Ruth and Nikki.
  Greetings, Nikki, Ruth, and Faye.
Greetings, dear and charming ladies,
  How are all of you today?

All my love I send, dear ladies,
  And I think of you each day:
Think of you, dear Ruth and Nikki—
  And of you, my dearest Faye!

ODE TO SPRING

Oh Spring,
Thou sudden, joyous thing!
Bright flowers thou dost bring;
The robin doth sing;
The meadow doth ring;
The ivy doth cling;
The bee's on the wing—
Bee, put up thy sting!
The kite's on the string;
Children do swing;
The baseball doth zing.
Oh Spring,
Have now thy fling!

MY TWO FRONT TEETH?

What do I want for Christmas?
  I find it hard to say.
There's nothing I can think of
  I need in any way.

I've little use for speakers
  With huge, pervasive sound—
Some precious peace and quiet
  I'd rather have around.

The latest high-tech gadget
  Do not present to me—
I have enough of living
  In thrall to gadgetry.

Don't give me a vacation
  To London, Paris, Rome—
What good to me is travel?
  My friends are here at home.

Nor would some gift X-rated
  Mean spicing up my life—
The spice I have already:
  A dear and loving wife.

With love and peace and friendship
  This Christmas, friend, I'm blessed . . .
And yet, could you but grant it,
  I'd make one slight request:

The future holds surprises—
  Let joy not disappear!
Let peace and love continue
  Throughout the coming year!

CONTENT WITH YOU

That, too, was good:
The white fog that descended
On the battered coast,
Cliffs, once hard and obstinate,
Now soft and yielding.
Offshore a foghorn blew,
And standing there with you
I felt no wayward urge.

Earlier we had seen
From that same high point
A herd of whales.
Rolling in unison
They made their way along,
Not veering from the path
Or varying their speed,
And I had felt the need
To steer a course like theirs.

Contentment follows urgency
As sunshine follows rain,
As peace follows war,
As silence follows speech.
For years, as each fair shape
Passed by, I stopped and turned—
Have I not earned
The right to be content?

Somewhere beyond the fog
The whales are rolling on
And shall do so until
Their kind itself is gone . . .
Whales on their migration,
Emerging into the sun,
Staying in formation,
Together moving as one.

LIKE MOONLIGHT ON THE SEA

The sky, grown dark, is clear tonight.
  The moon is high already.
Near full, it shines with soothing light—
  Subdued, and calm, and steady.

The ocean lures us, you and me—
  Intrepid would-be swimmers.
We watch, as on the restless sea
  The moonlight sways and shimmers.

What was it, then, not long ago
  That made you so suspicious?
The argument, which started slow,
  Grew quickly downright vicious. . . .

Like lashing, cold, wind-driven rain
  The stinging accusations.
Like anguished pleas to heaven, in vain
  The fumbling explanations.

At peace once more, this girl and boy
  Now face the dark Atlantic
And, moonstruck, kiss as they enjoy
  An interlude romantic.

Untroubled as the moon, dear wife,
  My love to introspection—
While on the restless sea of life
  Disturbed is love's reflection.

ORDINARY PEOPLE

When he talked
No ringing stunned your ear.
You could not know
That when he sang
The vast cathedral rang
Around, above, below . . .
That he could make
The chambers in his head resound,
His throat and larynx shake,
The lungs blast, the windpipe swell with sound.

And when she walked
No rhythm struck your eye.
You could not be aware
That when she danced
Each looker-on, entranced,
Sat forward in his chair . . .
That she could cause
Her arms to wave, her hips to sway
In such a manner as
Were you to see, would take your breath away.

TO EVERY STUDENT HERE
(To the tune of FROM EVERY KIND OF MAN, *from* THE MIKADO)

To every student here
  There's one thing I wish to say:
I'm the teacher—Is that quite clear?—
  And I determine who gets an "A".

You'd better prepare your lessons with care
If you want to receive an "A".

If you think that what's in store
  Is fluff, a holiday,
Well, you'd better just think once more
  If you expect to receive an "A".

Work, work, if you want to receive an "A"!
Work, work, if you want to receive an "A"!

I'm the expert: in my domain
  Authority I convey.
You'll agree if you've half a brain
  And you expect to receive an "A".

You'd better not make one single mistake
Or you'll never receive an "A".

As a scholar I'm simply grand,
  Full mastery I display—
As you'll show that you understand
  If you expect to receive an "A".

Work, work, if you want to receive an "A"!
Work, work, if you want to receive an "A"!

WORKIN' IN A WACKY WONDERLAND
(For company Christmas party)

What's that sound?
  Glasses clinkin'.
All around
  People drinkin'.
It's hip hip hooray,
We're happy today,
  Workin' in a wacky wonderland!

Ring-a-ling—
  Someone get it!
Hear it ring—
  Baby, let it!
To hell with the call—
We're havin' a ball,
  Workin' in a wacky wonderland!

In my office there's a small computer;
  I pretend it's Marilyn Monroe.
Wow! There's not a gal around that's cuter—
  If I were not so shy I'd tell her so.

By and by
  We'll grow tired—
Wonder why
  We're not fired?
Won't face that till last—
We're havin' a blast,
  Workin' in a wacky wonderland!

TO EVE

Let's go then, you and I, to where the ocean meets the sky,
Where no one's been before, a land that's neither wet nor dry.
  The beach, pristine, we'll comb;
  The shore, unsullied, roam;
We'll play all day in the ocean's spray, our clothing bits of
                                   foam.
Along the soft and sun-drenched sand, the shining sea in
                                   view,
Is where I'd like to run and frolic, laughing Eve, with you.

Let's follow where the river winds, through pleasant, shady
                                 groves,
By canyon walls and waterfalls and tranquil, sheltered coves.
  And if dark clouds portend
  A storm around the bend,
We'll wait, and know that there in time we'll find the
                           rainbow's end.
The rainbow's end—that farthest reach, where everything is
                                 new—
Is where I want to go exploring, unspoiled Eve, with you.

Together, dear, let's disappear—let's flee without a trace
To some exotic, some erotic, strange and distant place
  Of luscious, gorgeous sights
  And vast, intense delights,
Of blissful, glorious days and heavenly, still more blissful
                                 nights.
That place—that realm of pleasure, that Edenic Xanadu—
Is where I long to know enjoyment, lovely Eve, with you.

TRAFFIC JAM

The setting topographic:
  A long, extended hill,
A highway clogged with traffic;
  Three lanes, all standing still.

In front, behind, around us
  A sea of chrome and steel;
Its length and breadth astound us—
  The scene appears surreal.

Stuck, sitting in congestion
  Some thirty minutes straight,
We ask ourselves the question,
  "How long, then, must we wait?"

No word, no information.
  We try the radio—
Try station after station.
  Is any helpful? No.

What's going on, we wonder?
  Some failed, decrepit junk?
Some accident, some blunder,
  Some driver driving drunk?

Exasperated, fuming,
  Mid grumbling, groans and grunts,
We find ourselves assuming
  The worst. . . .   Then, all at once,

Commotion! What's occurring?
  May now some light be shed?
A sudden sound of whirring:
  A 'copter overhead.

Connection now we're making:
  The radio's voice is heard—
" . . . the story as it's breaking . . .
  " . . . an accident occurred . . . "

Another hour, they tell us,
  Before the road is cleared.
Bad timing, what befell us—
  But not as bad as feared.

We're not in any hurry.
  The outcome's not the best,
But glad we are that worry
  Has now been laid to rest.

Is not this rule conformant
  To what we know: in brief,
That ignorance is torment
  And knowledge is relief?

We wonder where we're going,
  And if it's good or bad.
The worst of all's not knowing—
  It's this that drives us mad.

That some Superior Being,
  Positioned in the sky,
All-compassing, all-seeing,
  Would beam us from on high

And show us our location,
  The picture from afar,
Reveal our situation
  And tell us where we are,

And tell us what we're facing,
  The truth about our state,
Toward what unknown we're racing,
  The nature of our fate!

We wish some Voice would clue us. . . .
  Still, say it did—What then?
Would any good it do us
  To know the Where and When?

No doubt, were we enlightened
  And should the news be good,
Our mood and spirits brightened
  Would soar, it's understood.

In joyous celebration
  We'd wave and stamp our feet
With shouts of jubilation
  And dancing in the street.

What if, though, unexpected,
  The news instead was bad:
We learn we weren't selected—
  Would that not make us sad?

Unsettled, dizzy, queasy,
  We'd ponder the abyss . . .
And think when life was easy
  And ignorance was bliss.

SO GLAD I FOUND YOU, DOMINIQUE

Such a long night, cold and lonely,
　　Emptiness with no relief,
Nothing—no emotion—only
　　Ache of unremitting grief.
Beauty, all that's most appealing,
　　Struck not one responsive spark:
When she died, so died all feeling,
　　Smothered as the world went dark.

Once her lovely, lilting laughter
　　Set my heart and mind aglow,
Promised joy forever after—
　　Goodness, that was long ago!
Once, adoring thoughts and wishes
　　Flamed in flashing, sparkling rhyme. . . .
All long gone, as dead as ashes,
　　Swept beneath the sands of time.

What will be? Were man omniscient
　　Who would dare to look ahead?
Yet were world and time sufficient
　　Little we would have to dread.
Neither world nor time's unbounded:
　　Might it not go on this way—
Inkling of relief unfounded,
　　Flat the skies ahead, and gray?

Come, the world could change tomorrow,
  Nothing ever stays the same.
Even in the midst of sorrow
  One must not give up the game.
Like a great volcano sleeping,
  Calm throughout its breadth and length,
My composure I've been keeping
  Even as I gather strength.

This I sense: my heart, so broken,
  Soon will lighten, soon will mend;
Then I'll feel my soul awaken,
  Feel the dark and coldness end.
More than likely this a feature:
  Such a change will be abrupt—
Oh, I'm like a force of nature,
  One just waiting to erupt!

Needed is the right occasion.
  What? Might this be close at hand?
Might the long-delayed explosion
  Happen sooner than I planned?
Something new I feel occurring:
  When I'm with you, Dominique,
Then I notice something stirring—
  Something's stirring as I speak.

Never, not in any city
  (And I've been to quite a few),
Have I met a girl as pretty,
  Girl as wonderful, as you!
Let me put my arms around you,
  Let me kiss you on the cheek—
I'm so happy that I found you,
  Dearest, dearest Dominique!

L'INVITATION AU VOYAGE
TO GIANNA, *Montreal 1998*

Noon! The morning's passed already,
　　Morning spent *à me bronzer*.
Warmth of sun on naked body—
　　Truly, *c'est la volupté*.
Here, reclining unsuspected,
　　Shielded from the neighbors' view,
Rising, falling undetected,
　　Half asleep I dream of you. . . .

Dream of you, my lovely Gianna,
　　See your dark Italian eyes,
See your smile—*che bella donna!*
　　What a beauty, what a prize!
Hear your laughter—*che dolcezza!*—
　　Music sweet to jaded ears,
Feel your warmth—*che gentilezza!*—
　　Such that I forget the years.

Years? A generation, rather.
　　What could bridge so wide a span?
Someone that could be your father—
　　How could he become your man?
No, for me—mere fancied lover—
　　Dear, you're like a luscious peach
Destined to remain forever
　　Fruit forbidden, out of reach.

Still, your ways are so entrancing,
   Never woman more *charmante.*
As for one—your way of dancing—
   Goodness, but it's *séduisante!*
Loved not Caesar Cleopatra?
   (*Cleo* was she called, or *Pat?*)
She sixteen. Here's looking at ya—
   Gianna, you are more than that!

Loved not Cleopatra Caesar,
   Virile still at fifty-four?
Didn't he know the way to please her—
   Lover, he whose child she bore?
So may you find me *aimable,*
   So may I ignite *ton coeur.*
Oh, I feel myself *capable*—
   Still at flood tide, *ma vigueur!*

Thus I'm being only truthful,
   Gianna darling, *je t'assure,*
When I term myself quite youthful,
   You, dear, on the whole *très mûre.*
Come, admit my case has merit:
   All the saints in heaven attest
You and I are close in spirit—
   Closer than our years suggest.

Therefore come, let's love each other—
   Love untroubled, *chère enfant.*
Gianna, come, let's live together—
   Ça me rendrait si content.
Let me be your man, your lover,
   Let me drown in *ta beauté*—
So may I at last discover
   Luxe, calme et volupté.

TO A FRIEND HIKING IN DIFFICULT TERRAIN
TOWARD EVENING

Up steep ascents you've trudged, to heights suspended
  In cloud and snow.
Down wooded slopes, unrushed, the trail's descended
  To plains below.

Across wet fields you've tramped, a raw wind blowing
  The livelong day.
Through tangled thickets pushed where thorns were
  How hard the way!   growing—

Since that bright, hopeful moment when you started
  You've plodded on;
Often you had a mind to quit, downhearted,
  Hope all but gone.

And now the sun, near spent, is swiftly sinking:
  Aglow, the west.
You're tired—no wonder once again you're thinking
  You'd like to rest.

It's late; you can't help wishing you were stronger—
  Still, don't despair!
The worst is past, endure a little longer—
  You're almost there!

CPSIA information can be obtained
at www.ICGtesting.com
Printed in the USA
BVHW030523140821
614143BV00003B/197